Great Curries

Great Curries

Manisha Kanani

Photography by David Jordan

WHITECAP
BOOKS

To my mother and grandmother – who have taught me everything I know.

This edition first published in 1997 by Whitecap Books

Whitecap Books
351 Lynn Avenue
North Vancouver
British Columbia
Canada V7J 2C4

Produced by
Anness Publishing Inc.
27 West 20th Street
New York
NY 10011

ISBN 1 55110 611 6

Publisher: Joanna Lorenz
Senior Cookery Editor: Linda Fraser
In-house Editor: Anne Hildyard
Designer: Alan Marshall
Photographer: David Jordan
Food and props styling for photography: Judy Williams

AUTHOR'S ACKNOWLEDGMENTS
I would like to thank Girish Bhogra, Ketan Natalia, Judy Williams, David Jordan
and Meena Unarket, all of whom have helped in their own special way.
Thank you for helping turn a dream into a reality. Above all, I would like to
thank my family (especially my mum) for their patience, support and
encouragement throughout the last few months, and for tasting my numerous
creations with such enthusiasm. I'm sure they've all had enough of curries
for a while.
Manisha Kanani

Printed and bound in Hong Kong

1 3 5 7 9 10 8 6 4 2

CONTENTS

INTRODUCTION

The popularity of Indian food has continued to grow over the years and supermarkets are now selling a wide range of spices, vegetables and special ingredients. Cooking Indian food has never been easier.

There is a misconception that Indian food is time-consuming and difficult to cook. Nothing could be further from the truth. With a basic understanding of the spices and their influences, Indian cooking can be simple.

The secret of Indian cooking lies in the imaginative use of spices. Different cooking techniques bring out a different flavor from each spice. The combination of flavors and variety of tastes are endless. No other cuisine offers such a diverse spectrum of dishes.

There is no rigid structure to an Indian meal. All the dishes are served at once and the diners help themselves. A meal should have a good balance of moist and dry dishes, and bread and rice are always served, accompanied by poppadums and a selection of pickles and chutneys.

You will find some well-known restaurant favorites in this book such as Chicken Tikka Masala, and Mixed Vegetable Curry, together with some more innovative dishes, all of which illustrate the versatility of Indian cooking. There is nothing more satisfying than Indian food when it is freshly cooked at home. If you always believed that long, slow cooking methods and complicated preparations were essential to create the authentic tastes and aromas of Indian food then this book will prove to be a refreshing culinary experience – and allow you to enjoy cooking and eating in true Indian style.

Spices

It is the blending of spices, seasonings and flavorings that gives Indian food its character.

Bay leaves
These fragrant leaves are used in many meat and rice dishes (1).

Cardamom
These pods are green, black and creamy-beige, green being the most common. Whole pods used in rice and meat dishes to add flavor should not be eaten. Use black seeds in desserts (2).

Cayenne pepper
Sometimes called red pepper powder this is hot or very hot and widely used (3).

Cinnamon
Cinnamon is available whole or ground. The sticks are used for flavor and are not eaten (4).

Cloves
Cloves are used in spice mixtures such as garam masala, and in meat and rice dishes (5).

Coriander
One of the most popular spices, these small beige seeds are used whole and ground, giving a slightly sweet flavor. The leaves, known as cilantro, are used for flavoring and as a garnish (6).

Cumin
Available as whole dark brown seeds and ground. The whole seeds are often fried in oil, releasing a strong musky flavor and aroma (7).

Curry leaves
These aromatic leaves are the Indian version of bay leaves (8).

Curry powder
There are many variations of this spice mixture, varying in both flavor and color (9).

Dried chilies
These red chilies are often fried in oil to release their strong flavor. The small ones are the most pungent (10).

Fennel seeds
A small light green seed, similar in smell and taste to anise. They are used in many vegetable and meat dishes. Roasted fennel seeds are also eaten after a meal to freshen the mouth (11).

Fenugreek seeds
These small pungent seeds are used in spice mixtures (12).

Garam masala
This is the main spice mixture of Indian cooking. It is a hot and aromatic powder and is added at the end of cooking (13).

Garlic
Available fresh and ground, garlic is used for its strong flavor. The powder is mainly used in spice mixtures (14).

Ginger
Both fresh and ground ginger have a sharp refreshing flavor. Fresh ginger should be peeled before use (15).

Mint
Fresh mint has a very refreshing flavor and is used in making chutneys and raitas (16).

Mustard seeds
Whole black mustard seeds are added to hot oil to release a mild, nutty flavor. They are used with vegetables and beans (17).

Nutmeg
Whole and ground, nutmeg has a sweet, nutty flavor (18).

Paprika
A mild, sweet red powder, paprika adds color (19).

Peppercorns
Black peppercorns are used whole and ground. They are also used in garam masala (20).

Saffron
Saffron is the dried stigmas of the saffron crocus. It is used in savory and sweet dishes for its aroma and color (21).

Sesame seeds
Small and creamy-white with a rich, nutty flavor, these seeds are used in vegetable dishes and sprinkled as a garnish (22).

Tamarind
The tamarind pod is dried to form a dark brown, sticky pulp which is soaked in hot water, then strained before use. It has a strong, sour taste and is used in curries and chutneys (23).

Turmeric
Turmeric is a bright yellow powder and is primarily used for its coloring properties. Because of its strong, bitter flavor it should be used sparingly (24).

Vegetables

Indian cooking specializes in a hundred different ways of using vegetables, everything from cauliflower, potatoes and peas to the more exotic and unusual varieties of vegetables such as okra, bitter melons and eggplant. In the Indian cuisine, vegetables are indispensable.

Eggplant
Available in different varieties, the shiny deep purple eggplant is the most common and widely used variety in Indian cooking. Eggplant has a strong flavor with a slightly bitter taste and is sometimes sprinkled with a little salt to extract some of these bitter juices (1).

Bitter melons
One of the many very bitter vegetables often used in Indian cooking. This long, knobbly green vegetable comes from Kenya and has a strong, bitter taste. To prepare a melon, peel the ridged skin with a sharp knife, scrape away and discard the seeds and chop the flesh (2).

Cauliflower
A large round vegetable with creamy-white flowers and green leaves. This versatile vegetable is very popular in Indian cooking and is often combined with other vegetables (3).

Chilies
Chilies are small hot members of the capsicum family. There are many types, varying in shape, size, color and flavor. Some are hotter than others. They are used extensively in Indian cooking, particularly the fresh green chili. For a milder flavor, remove seeds before using (4).

Okra
Okra is one of the most popular Indian vegetables. These small green five-sided pods have a very distinctive flavor and a slightly sticky, pulpy texture when they are cooked (5).

Onions
A popular root vegetable belonging to the allium family, onions have a strong pungent flavor and aroma. Globe onions are the most commonly used variety for Indian cooking. Scallions are also used in some dishes to add color and for their mild taste (6).

Bell peppers
Bell peppers are large hollow pods belonging to the capsicum family and come in a variety of colors. Red bell peppers are slightly sweeter than green bell peppers. They are used in a variety of Indian dishes, adding color and flavor (7).

Spinach
Available all year round, this green leafy vegetable has a mild delicate flavor. The leaves do vary in size but only the large thick leaves need to be trimmed of their stalks. Spinach is a popular vegetable in Indian cooking where it is cooked in many ways, both with meat and other vegetables (8).

Corn
Corn originated in America but is now grown all over the world. It has a delicious sweet, juicy flavor which is at its best just after picking (9).

Tomatoes
Tomatoes are available all year round in a variety of colors ranging from red to orange, yellow to green. They are an essential ingredient in Indian cooking and are widely used to make all sorts of sauces, chutneys and relishes (10).

Beans, Lentils and Rice

Beans and lentils play an important role in Indian cooking and are a good source of protein. Some are cooked whole, some are puréed and made into soups or "dals" and some are combined with vegetables or meat. Rice is always served as part of an Indian meal.

Black-eyed peas
Small cream-colored peas that have a black spot or "eye". They have a thinner skin than many other peas. When cooked they have a tender, creamy texture and a mildly smoky flavor. Black-eyed peas are widely used in Indian cooking (1).

Chick-peas
These round beige-colored beans have a strong, nutty flavor when they are cooked. As well as being used for curries, chick-peas are also ground into a flour which is widely used in many Indian dishes such as pakoras and bhajees (2).

Channa dal
Channa dal is very similar to yellow split peas but smaller in size and with a slightly sweeter taste. It is used in a variety of vegetable dishes and can also be deep-fried and mixed with Indian chips and spices such as in Bombay mix (3).

Small cannellini beans
Small oval beans which are either white or pale green in color. They have a very mild, refreshing flavor (4).

Green lentils or split peas
Also known as continental lentils, these have quite a strong flavor and retain their shape during cooking. Green lentils are extremely versatile and are used in a large number of Indian dishes (5).

Navy beans
Small, white oval beans which come in different varieties. Navy beans are ideal for Indian cooking because not only do they retain their shape but they also absorb the flavors of the spices well (6).

Kidney beans
Kidney beans are one of the most popular beans used in Indian cooking. They are dark red-brown, kidney-shaped beans with a strong flavor (7).

Mung beans
These are small, round green beans with a slightly sweet flavor and creamy texture. When sprouted they produce the familiar beansprouts. Split mung beans are also used in Indian cooking and often cooked with rice to make a popular Gujarati dish (8).

Rice
An annual cereal grass with many varieties. Different types of rice produce a different texture when cooked. Basmati rice is the most popular type eaten with Indian food. The long, slender grains have a distinctive and aromatic flavor (9).

Wash all varieties of rice in several changes of water and allow to soak before cooking. Rice can be cooked either by the absorption method, whereby the rice is cooked in a measured amount of liquid or, by the boiling method in which the rice is cooked in plenty of boiling water and then drained.

Yellow lentils
A dull orange-colored split pea with a distinctive earthy flavor. Yellow lentils are available plain and in an oily variety (10).

Red split lentils
A readily available lentil that can be used in place of yellow lentils for making dal (11).

SOAKING AND COOKING TIPS

Most dried beans, except lentils, need to be soaked overnight before cooking. Wash the beans thoroughly and remove any small stones and damaged beans. Put into a large bowl and cover with plenty of cold water. When cooking, allow double the volume of water to beans and boil for 10 minutes. This initial boiling period is essential to remove any harmful toxins. Drain, rinse and cook in fresh water. The cooking time for all beans varies, depending on the type and their freshness. Beans can be cooked in a pressure cooker to save time. Lentils, on the whole, do not need soaking. They should be washed in several changes of cold water before being cooked.

Breads

Breads are an integral part of any Indian meal. Most traditional Indian breads are unleavened, that is, they do not contain any rising agent, and are made with ground whole wheat flour, known as chapati flour or *atta*. Some are dry-cooked on a griddle, some are fried with a little oil, others are deep-fried to make small savory puffs. To enjoy Indian breads at their best, they should be made just before a meal and eaten hot.

Chapati

This is the staple bread of northern and central India. Chapatis or *rotis* are very thin, flat, unleavened bread made from ground whole wheat flour. They are cooked on a hot *tava*, which is a concave-shaped Indian griddle. Chapatis have a light texture and are fairly bland in taste, but spices added with the flour give more flavor (1).

Nan

Nan is a type of Indian bread. This large tear-shaped bread is traditionally baked in a tandoor oven, although it can also be broiled. Nan is normally made with flour enriched with yogurt and yeast, and can be eaten with most meat or vegetable dishes. There are many varieties of nan bread: plain nan, cilantro and garlic nan, and masala nan (2).

Paratha

A paratha is similar to the chapati except that it contains ghee (clarified butter), which gives the bread a flaky texture. They are much thicker than chapatis and are shallow fried as opposed to dry-cooked. Plain parathas are often eaten for lunch and go well with most vegetable dishes. Parathas can also be stuffed with various fillings, the most popular being spiced potato, and are generally served on their own (3).

Poori

A small deep-fried puffy bread made from ground whole wheat flour. Pooris are best eaten hot and are traditionally served for breakfast. They can be simply plain or flavored with spices such as cumin, turmeric and chili powder which are mixed into the dough. When served with a vegetable or fish curry, they make a perfect light snack or starter (4).

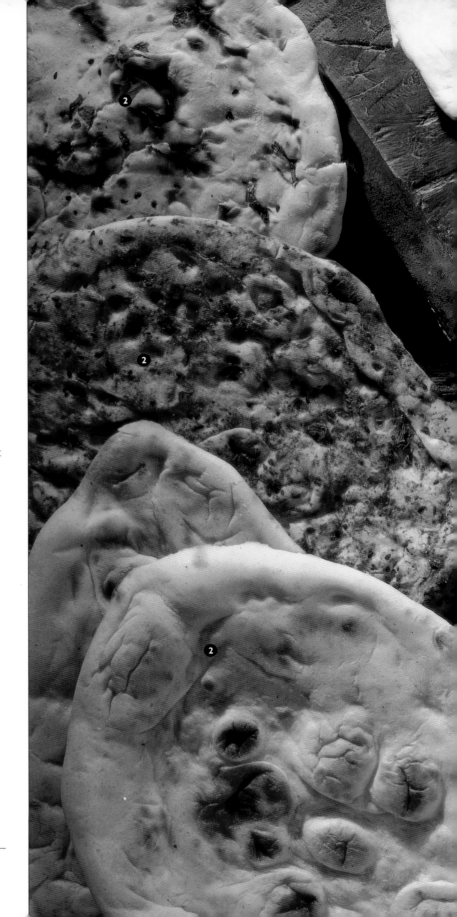

Curry Powder

Curry powders do not exist in India. Most traditional Indian households use individual spices which are freshly ground and mixed, when they are needed. There are many commercially blended curry powders available but it is just as easy to make your own. This is a basic recipe for a mild curry powder but you can adjust the quantities to suit your taste.

Makes about 1¹/₄ cups

INGREDIENTS
WHOLE SPICES
¹/₂ cup coriander seeds
4 tablespoons cumin seeds
2 tablespoons fennel seeds
2 tablespoons fenugreek seeds
4 dried red chilies
5 curry leaves

GROUND SPICES
1 tablespoon cayenne pepper
1 tablespoon turmeric
¹/₂ teaspoon salt

1 Dry-roast the whole spices in a large heavy-based frying pan for 8–10 minutes, shaking the pan from side to side until the spices begin to darken and release a rich aroma. Allow them to cool slightly.

2 Put the spices in a spice grinder and grind to a fine powder.

COOK'S TIP

If you would like a hot curry powder, increase the quantity of dried red chilies.

3 Add the remaining ground spices and store in an airtight jar.

Garam Masala

Garam means "hot" and masala means "spices" so the spices used are those which "heat" the body, such as black peppercorns, cinnamon and cloves. Garam masala is added at the end of cooking and sprinkled over dishes as a garnish.

Makes about 6 tablespoons

INGREDIENTS
10 dried red chilies
3 x 1-inch cinnamon sticks
2 curry leaves
2 tablespoons coriander seeds
2 tablespoons cumin seeds
1 teaspoon black peppercorns
1 teaspoon cloves
1 teaspoon fenugreek seeds
1 teaspoon black mustard seeds
¹/₄ teaspoon cayenne pepper

1 Dry-roast the chilies, cinnamon sticks and curry leaves in a large heavy-based frying pan for 2 minutes.

2 Add the coriander and cumin seeds, peppercorns, cloves, fenugreek and mustard seeds and dry-roast for another 8–10 minutes, shaking the pan from side to side until the spices begin to darken and release a rich aroma.

COOK'S TIP

The curry powder and garam masala will keep for 2–4 months in an airtight container. As with all spice mixes, the flavors will mature during storage.

3 Allow the mixture to cool slightly before grinding, then put the spices into a spice grinder or use a mortar and pestle and grind to a fine powder. Add the cayenne pepper, mix together and store the powder in an airtight jar.

Curry Paste

A curry paste is a "wet" blend of spices cooked with oil and vinegar which help to preserve the spices. It is a quick and convenient way of adding a mixture of spices.

Makes about 2¹/₂ cups

INGREDIENTS
¹/₂ cup coriander seeds
4 tablespoons cumin seeds
2 tablespoons fennel seeds
2 tablespoons fenugreek seeds
4 dried red chilies
5 curry leaves
1 tablespoon cayenne pepper
1 tablespoon ground turmeric
²/₃ cup white wine vinegar
1 cup oil

COOK'S TIP
Once the paste has been cooked, heat a little more oil and pour on top of the paste in the jar. This will help to preserve the paste and prevent any mold from forming.

1 Put all the whole spices into a spice grinder or mortar and pestle and grind to a fine powder. Spoon into a bowl and add the remaining ground spices.

2 Mix all the ground spices with the vinegar and add 5 tablespoons water to form a thin paste.

3 Heat the oil in a large heavy-based frying pan and stir-fry the spice paste for 10 minutes or until all the water has been absorbed. When the oil rises to the surface the paste is cooked. Allow to cool slightly before spooning into sterilized jars.

Tikka Paste

A delicious, versatile paste which can be used in a variety of dishes such as Chicken Tikka Masala. This is a spicy paste with a slightly sour flavor.

Makes about 2 cups

INGREDIENTS
2 tablespoons coriander seeds
2 tablespoons cumin seeds
1¹/₂ tablespoons garlic powder
2 tablespoons paprika
1 tablespoon garam masala
1 tablespoon ground ginger
2 teaspoons cayenne pepper
¹/₂ teaspoon ground turmeric
1 tablespoon dried mint
¹/₄ teaspoon salt
1 teaspoon lemon juice
a few drops of red food coloring
a few drops of yellow food coloring
²/₃ cup white wine vinegar
²/₃ cup oil

1 Put the coriander and cumin seeds into a spice grinder or use a mortar and pestle and grind to a fine powder. Spoon the spice mixture into a bowl and add the ground spices, mint and salt, stirring the mixture well.

2 Mix the spice powder with the lemon juice, food colorings and vinegar and add 2 tablespoons water to form a thin paste.

3 Heat the oil in a large heavy-based frying pan and stir-fry the paste for 10 minutes or until all the water has been absorbed. When the oil rises to the surface the paste is cooked. Allow the paste to cool slightly before spooning into sterilized jars.

TECHNIQUES

Skinning and Chopping Tomatoes

This is a very simple and easy way of preparing tomatoes for cooking and relishes.

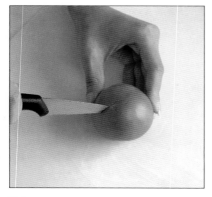

1 Using a small sharp knife, cut a small cross on the bottom of each tomato.

2 Put the tomatoes in a bowl and pour over boiling water. Let stand 20–30 seconds until the skin splits. Drain and transfer to a bowl of cold water.

3 Peel off the skin and chop finely.

Seeding and Chopping Chilies

Try using a fork and knife when preparing chilies to prevent your hands from burning.

1 Trim the chilies at both ends.

2 Cut the chilies in half lengthwise.

COOK'S TIP
If you have sensitive skin, wear a pair of rubber gloves.

3 Scrape away and discard the seeds, using the tip of the knife, and finely chop the flesh of the chilies.

Chopping Onions

A quick and easy way of cutting onions.

1 Cut the onion in half, leaving the root intact and peel off the outer skin.

2 Place the cut side down and make horizontal cuts at ¼-inch intervals, making sure not to cut through the root.

3 Make vertical cuts in the same way at ¼-inch intervals.

4 Hold the onion firmly with one hand and carefully chop finely.

Preparing Fresh Ginger

Fresh ginger is very simple to prepare.

1 Break off a small piece of ginger and remove any rough ends.

2 Peel off the tough skin, using a small sharp knife or potato peeler.

3 Cut the ginger into thin slices and chop finely.

COOK'S TIP

Alternatively, you can make ginger purée in a food processor or blender and freeze it in ice-cube trays. Once frozen, seal in a plastic bag. The purée will keep in the freezer for up to 2 months.

DIPS AND RELISHES

Cucumber Raita

A cool, refreshing relish, ideal with curries or served as a dip with dishes such as kebabs.

Makes about 2½ cups

INGREDIENTS
½ cucumber
1 green chili, seeded and
    finely chopped
1¼ cups plain yogurt
¼ teaspoon salt
¼ teaspoon ground cumin

1 Dice the cucumber finely and place in a bowl. Add the chili.

2 Beat the yogurt with a fork until smooth and stir into the cucumber and chili mixture.

3 Stir in the salt and cumin. Cover and chill before serving.

VARIATION
Instead of cucumber, you can use two skinned, seeded and chopped tomatoes and 1 tablespoon chopped cilantro.

Tomato and Chili Chutney

If you like hot food, this spicy tomato chutney is the perfect accompaniment.

Makes about 2 cups

INGREDIENTS
4 tomatoes
1 red pepper
2 green chilies, roughly chopped
1 garlic clove, roughly chopped
¼ teaspoon salt
½ teaspoon sugar
1 teaspoon cayenne pepper
3 tablespoons tomato paste
1 tablespoon chopped cilantro

1 Roughly chop the tomatoes.

2 Halve the red pepper and remove the core and seeds. Roughly chop the red pepper halves.

3 Put all the ingredients into a food processor or blender together with 2 tablespoons water and process until fairly smooth. Cover and chill.

Cilantro Chutney

A popular Indian side dish, this delicious chutney is made using cilantro.

Makes about 2 cups

INGREDIENTS
4 ounces cilantro leaves
1 green chili
2 garlic cloves, roughly chopped
1 teaspoon salt
$^1/_2$ teaspoon sugar
$1^1/_2$ tablespoons lemon juice
3 tablespoons ground peanuts

1 Roughly chop the cilantro leaves.

2 Seed and roughly chop the chili.

3 Put all the ingredients into a food processor or blender together with $^1/_2$ cup water and process until smooth. Cover and chill.

Mint and Coconut Chutney

This mild chutney has a delicious strong flavor.

Makes about $1^1/_2$ cups

INGREDIENTS
2 ounces fresh mint leaves
6 tablespoons dried coconut
1 tablespoon sesame seeds
$^1/_4$ teaspoon salt
$^3/_4$ cup plain yogurt

COOK'S TIP
This chutney can be made in advance and will keep for up to five days in the fridge.

1 Roughly chop the mint.

2 Put all the ingredients into a food processor or blender and process until smooth. Cover and chill.

Rogan Josh

The most popular of all lamb dishes, the lamb is traditionally marinated in yogurt then cooked with spices and tomatoes which gives the dish its rich, red appearance.

Serves 4

INGREDIENTS
2 pounds lamb fillet
3 tablespoons lemon juice
1 cup plain yogurt
1 teaspoon salt
2 garlic cloves, crushed
1-inch piece ginger root, grated
4 tablespoons oil
½ teaspoon cumin seeds
2 bay leaves
4 green cardamom pods
1 onion, finely chopped
2 teaspoons ground coriander
2 teaspoons ground cumin
1 teaspoon cayenne pepper
14-ounce can chopped tomatoes
2 tablespoons tomato paste
toasted cumin seeds and bay leaves,
    to garnish
plain rice, to serve

water

chopped tomatoes • oil • onion

garlic • plain yogurt • ground cumin • tomato paste

lemon juice • ground coriander

cayenne pepper • salt • cumin seeds • lamb fillet

ginger • bay leaves • cardamom pods

1 Trim away any excess fat from the meat and cut into 1-inch cubes.

2 In a bowl, mix together the lemon juice, yogurt, salt, 1 garlic clove and the ginger. Add the lamb and leave in the marinade overnight.

3 Heat the oil in a large frying pan and fry the cumin seeds for 2 minutes or until they begin to sputter. Add the bay leaves and cardamom pods and fry for another 2 minutes.

4 Add the onion and remaining garlic and fry for 5 minutes. Stir in the ground coriander, cumin and cayenne pepper and fry for 2 minutes.

5 Add the marinated lamb and cook for 5 minutes, stirring occasionally.

6 Add the tomatoes, tomato paste and ⅔ cup water. Bring to a boil then reduce the heat. Cover and simmer for about 1–1½ hours or until the meat is tender. Serve with plain rice and garnish with toasted cumin seeds and bay leaves.

Matar Keema

One of the simplest Indian dishes to make. This spicy lamb curry can also be used as a tasty filling for stuffing vegetables such as peppers and large beefsteak tomatoes.

Serves 4

INGREDIENTS
3 tablespoons oil
1 onion, finely chopped
2 garlic cloves, crushed
1-inch piece ginger root, grated
2 green chilies, finely chopped
1½ pounds ground lamb
1 teaspoon ground cumin
1 teaspoon ground coriander
1 teaspoon cayenne pepper
1 teaspoon salt
6 ounces frozen peas, thawed
2 tablespoons lemon juice
nan bread and plain yogurt,
    to serve

cayenne pepper

ground cumin

frozen peas

oil

ground lamb

lemon juice   *garlic*   *green chilies*

ground coriander   *ginger*   *salt*   *onion*

1 Heat the oil in a large saucepan and fry the onion for 5 minutes, until golden brown. Add the garlic, ginger and chilies and fry for 2–3 minutes.

2 Add the minced lamb and stir-fry for about 5 minutes.

3 Stir in the ground cumin, ground coriander, cayenne pepper and salt with 1¼ cups water. Cover and simmer for about 25 minutes.

4 Add the peas and lemon juice. Cook for another 10 minutes, uncovered, or until the meat is tender. Serve with nan bread and plain yogurt.

Lamb with Apricots

Lamb is combined with apricots and traditional Indian spices to produce a rich, spicy curry with a hint of sweetness.

Serves 4

INGREDIENTS
2 pounds stewing lamb
2 tablespoons oil
1-inch cinnamon stick
4 green cardamom pods
1 onion, chopped
1 tablespoon curry paste
1 teaspoon ground cumin
1 teaspoon ground coriander
¼ teaspoon salt
6 ounces ready-to-eat dried apricots
1½ cups lamb broth
yellow rice and mango chutney,
    to serve
cilantro, to garnish

lamb broth

ground cumin

onion

curry paste

oil

dried apricots

stewing lamb

salt

ground coriander

cardamom pods

cinnamon stick

1 Remove any visible fat and cut the meat into 1-inch cubes.

2 Heat the oil in a large saucepan and fry the cinnamon stick and cardamoms for 2 minutes. Add the onion and fry for about 6–8 minutes.

3 Add the curry paste and fry for 2 minutes. Stir in the cumin, coriander and salt and fry for 2–3 minutes.

4 Add the meat, apricots and the broth. Cover and cook for 1–1½ hours. Serve on yellow rice with the chutney in a separate bowl. Garnish with cilantro.

Beef Madras

Madras curries originatd in southern India. They are aromatic, robust and pungent in flavor. This recipe uses beef but you can replace this with lamb, if you prefer.

Serves 4

INGREDIENTS
2 pounds stewing beef
3 tablespoons oil
1 large onion, finely chopped
4 cloves
4 green cardamom pods
2 green chilies, finely chopped
1-inch piece ginger root,
    finely chopped
2 garlic cloves, crushed
2 dried red chilies
1 tablespoon curry paste
2 teaspoons ground coriander
1 teaspoon ground cumin
½ teaspoon salt
⅔ cup beef broth
tomato rice, to serve
cilantro, to garnish

garlic *ginger* *onion*

beef broth *stewing beef*

curry paste

oil *ground cumin*

ground coriander *salt* *cloves* *cardamom pods* *red chilies* *green chilies*

1 Remove any visible fat and cut the meat into 1-inch cubes.

2 Heat the oil in a large frying pan and fry the onion, cloves and cardamom pods for 5 minutes. Add the fresh green chilies, ginger, garlic and dried chilies and fry for a further 2 minutes.

3 Add the curry paste and fry for about 2 minutes. Add the beef and fry for 5–8 minutes until all the meat pieces are lightly browned.

4 Add the coriander, cumin, salt and broth. Cover and simmer gently for 1–1½ hours or until the meat is tender. Serve with tomato rice and garnish with a sprig of cilantro.

Lamb Meatballs

Aromatic spices are combined with ground meat to produce authentic Indian-style meatballs.

Serves 4

INGREDIENTS

FOR THE MEATBALLS
1½ pounds ground lamb
1 green chili, roughly chopped
1 garlic clove, chopped
1-inch piece ginger root, chopped
¼ teaspoon garam masala
¼ teaspoon salt
3 tablespoons chopped cilantro

FOR THE SAUCE
2 tablespoons oil
½ teaspoon cumin seeds
1 onion, chopped
1 garlic clove, chopped
1-inch piece ginger root,
    finely chopped
1 teaspoon ground cumin
1 teaspoon ground coriander
½ teaspoon salt
½ teaspoon cayenne pepper
1 tablespoon tomato paste
14-ounce can chopped tomatoes
cilantro rice, to serve
cilantro, to garnish

chopped
tomatoes

green chili

garlic

cayenne
pepper

ginger

oil

ground
coriander

tomato
paste

garam
masala

ground
cumin

cumin
seeds

onion

ground lamb

fresh coriander

1 To make the meatballs, put all the ingredients into a food processor or blender and process until the mixture binds together.

2 Shape the mixture into 16 balls. Cover and chill for 10 minutes.

3 To make the sauce, heat the oil and fry the cumin seeds until they sputter. Add the onion, garlic and ginger and fry for 5 minutes. Stir in the remaining sauce ingredients and simmer for 5 minutes.

COOK'S TIP

You can make the meatballs the day before. Cover with plastic wrap and store in the fridge until needed.

4 Add the meatballs. Bring to a boil, cover and simmer for 25–30 minutes or until the meatballs are cooked through. Serve on cilantro rice and garnish with cilantro sprigs.

Beef Vindaloo

A fiery hot dish originally from Goa, a "vindaloo" curry is made using a unique blend of hot aromatic spices and vinegar to give it a distinctive spicy flavor.

Serves 4

INGREDIENTS

1 tablespoon cumin seeds
4 dried red chilies
1 teaspoon black peppercorns
5 green cardamom pods, seeds only
1 teaspoon fenugreek seeds
1 teaspoon black mustard seeds
½ teaspoon salt
½ teaspoon brown sugar
4 tablespoons white wine vinegar
4 tablespoons oil
1 large onion, finely chopped
2 pounds stewing beef, cut into
   1-inch cubes
1-inch piece ginger root,
   finely chopped
1 garlic clove, crushed
2 teaspoons ground coriander
½ teaspoons ground turmeric
plain and yellow rice, to serve

1 Put the cumin seeds, chilies, peppercorns, cardamom seeds, fenugreek seeds and mustard seeds into a spice grinder or use a mortar and pestle and grind to a fine powder. Add the salt, sugar and white wine vinegar and mix to a thin paste.

2 Heat 2 tablespoons of the oil in a large frying pan and fry the onions for 10 minutes. Put the onions and the spice mixture into a food processor or blender and process to a coarse paste.

3 Heat the remaining oil in the frying pan and fry the meat cubes for about 10 minutes, until lightly browned. Remove the beef cubes with a slotted spoon and set aside.

4 Add the ginger and garlic and fry for 2 minutes. Stir in the ground coriander and turmeric and fry for 2 minutes.

5 Add the spice and onion paste and fry for about 5 minutes.

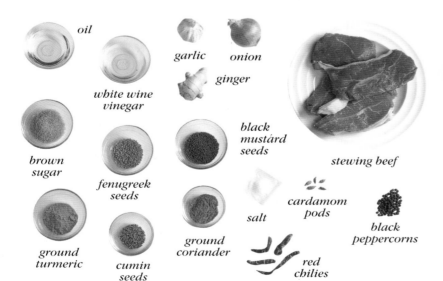

oil

garlic *onion*

ginger

white wine vinegar

black mustard seeds

stewing beef

brown sugar

fenugreek seeds

salt

cardamom pods

black peppercorns

ground turmeric *cumin seeds* *ground coriander*

red chilies

6 Return the meat to the pan together with 1¼ cups water. Cover and simmer for 1–1½ hours or until the meat is tender. Serve with plain and yellow rice.

COOK'S TIP
To make plain and yellow rice, infuse a pinch of saffron strands or dissolve a little ground turmeric in 1 tablespoon hot water. Stir into half the cooked rice until uniformly yellow. Carefully mix the yellow rice into the plain rice.

Lamb Kebabs

First introduced by the Muslims, kebabs have now become a favorite Indian dish.

Serves 4

INGREDIENTS

FOR THE KEBABS
2 pounds ground lamb
1 large onion, roughly chopped
2-inch piece ginger root, chopped
2 garlic cloves, crushed
1 green chili, finely chopped
1 teaspoon cayenne pepper
2 tablespoons chopped
   cilantro
1 teaspoon garam masala
2 teaspoons ground coriander
1 teaspoon ground cumin
1 teaspoon salt
1 egg, beaten
1 tablespoon plain yogurt
1 tablespoon oil
mixed salad leaves, to serve

FOR THE RAITA
1 cup plain yogurt
½ cucumber, finely chopped
2 tablespoons chopped fresh mint
¼ teaspoon salt

1 Put all the ingredients for the kebabs, except the yogurt and oil, into a food processor or blender and process until the mixture makes a paste. Spoon into a bowl and let marinate for 1 hour.

2 For the sauce, mix together all the ingredients and chill for 15 minutes.

cucumber garlic

plain
yogurt

garam
masala

ground
cumin ground
coriander ground lamb

cayenne
pepper cilantro egg onion ginger mint green
chili

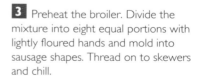

3 Preheat the broiler. Divide the mixture into eight equal portions with lightly floured hands and mold into sausage shapes. Thread on to skewers and chill.

4 Brush the kebabs lightly with the yogurt and oil and cook under a hot broiler for 8–10 minutes, turning occasionally, until brown all over. Serve the kebabs over mixed salad leaves accompanied by the raita.

Balti Beef

Balti curries are cooked and served in a two-handled pan known as a karahi and are traditionally served with nan bread. If you don't have a karahi then you can use a wok.

Serves 4

INGREDIENTS
1 red bell pepper
1 green bell pepper
2 tablespoons oil
1 teaspoon cumin seeds
½ teaspoon fennel seeds
1 onion, cut into thick wedges
1 garlic clove, crushed
1-inch piece ginger root,
    finely chopped
1 red chilli, finely chopped
1 tablespoon curry paste
½ teaspoon salt
1½ pounds rump or fillet steak, cut
    into thick strips
cilantro nan bread, to serve

oil   *fennel seeds*   *green bell pepper*

curry paste   *red bell pepper*

red chili   *onion*   *steak*

cumin seeds   *salt*   *ginger*

garlic

1 Cut the red and green bell peppers into 1-inch chunks.

2 Heat the oil in a wok or karahi and fry the cumin and fennel seeds for about 2 minutes or until they begin to sputter. Add the onion, garlic, ginger and chili and fry for 5 minutes.

3 Add the curry paste and salt and fry for another 3–4 minutes.

4 Add the bell peppers and stir-fry for about 5 minutes. Stir in the beef and continue to fry for 10–12 minutes or until the meat is tender. Serve with warm cilantro nan bread.

Spicy Lamb and Potato Stew

Transform this simple dish into a tasty stew with the addition of Indian spices.

Serves 4

INGREDIENTS

1½ pounds lamb fillet
3 tablespoons oil
1 onion, finely chopped
2 bay leaves
1 green chili, seeded and
    finely chopped
2 garlic cloves, finely chopped
2 teaspoons ground coriander
1 teaspoon ground cumin
½ teaspoon ground turmeric
½ teaspoon cayenne pepper
½ teaspoon salt
8 ounces tomatoes, peeled and
    finely chopped
2½ cups lamb broth
2 large potatoes, cut into
    1-inch chunks
chopped cilantro, to garnish
chapatis, to serve

potatoes

lamb broth

oil

tomatoes
onion

ground
turmeric

ground
cumin

cayenne
pepper

lamb fillet

salt

garlic

bay
leaves

ground
coriander

green chili

1 Remove any visible fat and cut the meat into 1-inch cubes.

2 Heat the oil in a large saucepan and fry the onion, bay leaves, chili and garlic for 5 minutes.

3 Add the meat and cook for about 6–8 minutes, until lightly browned.

4 Add the ground coriander, cumin, turmeric, cayenne pepper and salt and cook for 3–4 minutes, stirring constantly to prevent the spices from sticking.

5 Add the tomatoes and broth and simmer for 5 minutes, until the sauce thickens. Bring to a boil, cover and simmer for 1 hour.

6 Add the potatoes and cook for another 30–40 minutes or until the meat is tender. Garnish with chopped cilantro and serve with chapatis.

Chicken Tikka Masala

Tender chicken pieces cooked in a creamy, spicy tomato sauce and served on nan bread.

Serves 4

INGREDIENTS

1½ pounds chicken breasts, skinned
6 tablespoons tikka paste
4 tablespoons plain yogurt
2 tablespoons oil
1 onion, chopped
1 garlic clove, crushed
1 green chili, seeded and chopped
1-inch piece ginger root, grated
1 tablespoon tomato paste
1 tablespoon ground almonds
1 cup water
3 tablespoons butter, melted
¼ cup heavy cream
1 tablespoon lemon juice
cilantro sprigs, plain yogurt and
    toasted cumin seeds,
    to garnish
nan bread, to serve

onion

oil

heavy
cream

butter

tikka
paste

chicken breasts

ginger

plain
yogurt

lemon juice

green chili

garlic

ground
almonds

tomato
paste

1 Cut the chicken into 1-inch cubes. Put 3 tablespoons of the tikka paste and all of the yogurt into a bowl. Add the chicken and let marinate for 20 minutes.

2 For the tikka sauce, heat the oil and fry the onion, garlic, chili and ginger for 5 minutes. Add remaining tikka paste and fry for 2 minutes. Add the tomato paste, almonds and water, simmer 15 minutes.

3 Meanwhile, thread the chicken onto wooden skewers. Preheat the broiler.

4 Brush the chicken pieces with the butter and broil under medium heat for 15 minutes, turning occasionally.

5 Put the tikka sauce into a food processor or blender and process until smooth. Return to the pan.

6 Add the cream and lemon juice, remove the chicken pieces from the skewers and add to the saucepan, then simmer for 5 minutes. Serve on nan bread and garnish with cilantro, yogurt and toasted cumin seeds.

COOK'S TIP
Soak the wooden skewers in cold water before using to prevent them from burning while broiling.

Tandoori Chicken

This classic Indian dish is traditionally cooked in the tandoor which is a vat-shaped clay oven, heated with charcoal or wood.

Serves 4

INGREDIENTS
8 chicken pieces, such as thighs, drumsticks, and halved breasts, skinned
4 tablespoons lemon juice
1 teaspoon salt
2 garlic cloves, roughly chopped
1-inch piece ginger root, roughly chopped
2 green chilies, roughly chopped
¾ cup plain yogurt
1 teaspoon salt
1 teaspoon cayenne pepper
1 teaspoon garam masala
1 teaspoon ground cumin
1 teaspoon ground coriander
red food coloring (optional)
2 tablespoons butter, melted
lemon wedges, to garnish
cayenne pepper and a sprig of fresh mint, to garnish
salad and Cucumber Raita, to serve

plain yogurt

ground cumin

chicken pieces

red food coloring

ground coriander

butter

ginger

green chili

garam masala

lemon juice

cayenne pepper

garlic

1 Cut deep slashes in the chicken pieces. Mix together the lemon juice and the salt and rub over the chicken. Let marinate for 10 minutes.

2 Put the garlic, ginger and chilies into a food processor or blender and process until smooth. Add the garlic mixture to a bowl containing the yogurt, salt, cayenne pepper, garam masala, ground cumin and ground coriander.

3 Brush the chicken pieces with food coloring and put into a dish. Add the marinade and chill overnight. Preheat the oven to 425°F. Put the chicken in a roasting pan and bake for 40 minutes, basting with butter. Serve with lemon, salad, and Cucumber Raita, garnished with cayenne pepper and mint.

COOK'S TIP

The traditional bright red color associated with this dish is derived from food coloring. This is only optional and may be omitted from the recipe if you wish.

Coconut Chicken

A Goan-style curry made from a delicious blend
of authentic Indian spices and toasted coconut.

Serves 4

INGREDIENTS

1½ cups dried coconut
2 tablespoons oil
½ teaspoon cumin seeds
4 black peppercorns
1 tablespoon fennel seeds
1 tablespoon coriander seeds
2 onions, finely chopped
½ teaspoon salt
8 small chicken pieces, such as
    thighs and drumsticks, skinned
cilantro sprigs and lemon wedges,
    to garnish
Mint and Coconut Chutney,
    to serve

coriander
seeds

dried
coconut

oil

chicken pieces

fennel seeds

cumin
seeds

black
peppercorns

salt

onions

1 Put the dried coconut in a bowl
with 3 tablespoons water. Let soak for
15 minutes.

2 Meanwhile, heat 1 tablespoon of the
oil in a large frying pan and fry the cumin
seeds, peppercorns, fennel and coriander
seeds over low heat for 3–4 minutes
until the seeds begin to sputter.

3 Add the finely chopped onions and
fry for about 5 minutes.

4 Stir in the coconut and salt and
continue to fry for another 5 minutes,
stirring occasionally to prevent the
mixture from sticking to the pan.

5 Put the coconut mixture into a food
processor or blender and process to
form a coarse paste. Spoon into a bowl
and set aside until required.

6 Heat the remaining oil and fry the chicken for 10 minutes. Add the coconut paste and cook over low heat for 15–20 minutes, or until the coconut mixture is golden brown and the chicken is tender. Garnish with sprigs of cilantro and lemon wedges and serve with Mint and Coconut Chutney.

COOK'S TIP
Make the spiced coconut mixture the day before and chill it in the fridge, then continue from the final step when required.

Chicken Dhansak

Dhansak curries originated in the Parsee community and are traditionally made with lentils and meat.

Serves 4

INGREDIENTS
½ cup green lentils
2 cups broth
3 tablespoons oil
1 teaspoon cumin seeds
2 curry leaves
1 onion, finely chopped
1-inch piece ginger root, chopped
1 green chili, finely chopped
1 teaspoon ground cumin
1 teaspoon ground coriander
¼ teaspoon salt
¼ teaspoon cayenne pepper
14-ounce can chopped tomatoes
8 chicken pieces, skinned
4 tablespoons chopped cilantro
1 teaspoon garam masala
cilantro sprigs, to garnish
plain and yellow rice, to serve

1 Rinse the lentils under cold running water. Put into a large heavy-based saucepan with the broth. Bring to a boil, cover and simmer for about 15–20 minutes. Drain and set aside.

2 Heat the oil in a large saucepan and fry the cumin seeds and curry leaves for 2 minutes. Add the onion, ginger and chili and fry for about 5 minutes. Stir in the cumin, coriander, salt and cayenne pepper with 2 tablespoons water.

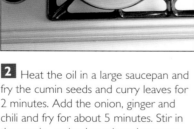

3 Add the tomatoes and the chicken. Cover and cook for 10–15 minutes.

4 Add the lentils and broth, cilantro and garam masala and cook for about 10 minutes or until the chicken is tender. Garnish with cilantro sprigs and serve with plain and yellow rice.

vegetable broth
ground cumin
oil
onion
ground coriander
cayenne pepper
chicken pieces
garam masala
cumin seeds
green lentils
chopped tomatoes
cilantro
curry leaves
green chili
ginger

Hot Chili Chicken

Not for the faint-hearted, this fiery, hot curry is made with a spicy chili masala paste.

Serves 4

INGREDIENTS
2 tablespoons tomato paste
2 garlic cloves, roughly chopped
2 green chilies, roughly chopped
5 dried red chilies
½ teaspoon salt
¼ teaspoon sugar
1 teaspoon cayenne pepper
½ teaspoon paprika
1 tablespoon curry paste
2 teaspoons oil
½ teaspoon cumin seeds
1 onion, finely chopped
2 bay leaves
1 teaspoon ground coriander
1 teaspoon ground cumin
¼ teaspoon ground turmeric
14-ounce can chopped tomatoes
⅔ cup water
8 chicken thighs, skinned
1 teaspoon garam masala
sliced green chilies, to garnish
chapatis and plain yogurt,
    to serve

chopped tomatoes

ground turmeric

ground coriander

curry paste

paprika   **chicken thighs**   **garlic**   **onion**

tomato paste

garam masala

cayenne pepper

ground cumin

cumin seeds

green chilies

bay leaves

red chilies

1 Put the tomato paste, garlic, green and dried red chilies, salt, sugar, cayenne pepper, paprika and curry paste into a food processor or blender and process to a smooth paste.

2 Heat the oil in a large saucepan and fry the cumin seeds for 2 minutes. Add the onion and bay leaves and fry for about 5 minutes.

3 Add the chilli paste and fry for 2–3 minutes. Add the remaining ground spices and cook for 2 minutes. Add the chopped tomatoes and water. Bring to a boil and simmer for 5 minutes or until the sauce thickens.

4 Add the chicken and garam masala. Cover and simmer for 25–30 minutes, until the chicken is tender. Serve with chapatis and plain yogurt, garnished with sliced green chilies.

Chicken Saag

A mildly spiced dish using a popular combination of spinach and chicken. This recipe is best made using fresh spinach, but if this is unavailable you can use frozen instead.

Serves 4

INGREDIENTS

8 ounces fresh spinach leaves,
    washed but not dried
1-inch piece ginger root, grated
2 garlic cloves, crushed
1 green chili, roughly chopped
scant 1 cup water
2 tablespoons oil
2 bay leaves
1/4 teaspoon black peppercorns
1 onion, finely chopped
4 tomatoes, peeled and
    finely chopped
2 teaspoons curry powder
1 teaspoon salt
1 teaspoon cayenne pepper
3 tablespoons plain yogurt
8 chicken thighs, skinned
plain yogurt and cayenne pepper,
    to garnish
masala nan, to serve

plain yogurt   *curry powder*   *cayenne pepper*

black peppercorns   *chicken thighs*   *ginger*

spinach leaves   *onion*   *green chili*   *bay leaves*   *tomatoes*   *garlic*

1 Cook the spinach, without water, in a tightly covered saucepan for 5 minutes. Put the spinach, ginger, garlic and chili with 1/4 cup of the water into a food processor or blender and process to a thick purée.

2 Heat the oil in a large saucepan, add the bay leaves and black peppercorns and fry for 2 minutes. Add the onion and fry for 6–8 minutes or until the onion has browned.

3 Add the tomatoes and simmer for about 5 minutes. Stir in the curry powder, salt and cayenne pepper and cook for 2 minutes.

4 Add the purée and 2/3 cup water; simmer for 5 minutes.

5 Add the yogurt, 1 tablespoon at a time, and simmer for 5 minutes.

6 Add the chicken. Cover and cook for 25–30 minutes or until the chicken is tender. Serve on masala nan, drizzle over some plain yogurt and dust with cayenne pepper.

Jeera Chicken

An aromatic dish with a delicious, distinctive taste of cumin. Serve simply with a salad and yogurt.

Serves 4

INGREDIENTS
3 tablespoons cumin seeds
3 tablespoons oil
½ teaspoon black peppercorns
4 green cardamom pods
2 green chilies, finely chopped
2 garlic cloves, crushed
1-inch piece ginger root, grated
1 teaspoon ground coriander
2 teaspoons ground cumin
½ teaspoon salt
8 chicken pieces, such as thighs and
    drumsticks, skinned
1 teaspoon garam masala
cilantro and cayenne pepper,
    to garnish
Cucumber Raita, to serve

oil

black peppercorns

chicken pieces

garam masala

ground coriander

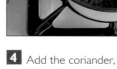
ground cumin

cumin seeds

ginger

green chilies

salt

garlic

green cardamom pods

cinnamon stick

1 Dry-roast 1 tablespoon of the cumin seeds for 5 minutes and set aside.

2 Heat the oil in a large saucepan and fry the remaining cumin seeds, black peppercorns and cardamoms for about 2–3 minutes.

3 Add the chilies, garlic and ginger and fry for 2 minutes.

4 Add the coriander, cumin and salt and cook for 2–3 minutes.

5 Add the chicken. Cover and simmer for 20–25 minutes.

6 Add the garam masala and reserved toasted cumin seeds and cook for another 5 minutes. Serve with Cucumber Raita, garnished with cayenne pepper and cilantro.

Balti Chicken Curry

Tender pieces of chicken are lightly cooked with fresh vegetables and aromatic spices in the traditional Balti style.

Serves 4

INGREDIENTS
1½ pounds chicken breasts, skinned
2 tablespoons oil
½ teaspoon cumin seeds
½ teaspoon fennel seeds
1 onion, thickly sliced
2 garlic cloves, crushed
1-inch piece ginger root,
    finely chopped
1 tablespoon curry paste
8 ounces broccoli, broken
    into florets
4 tomatoes, cut into thick wedges
1 teaspoon garam masala
2 tablespoons chopped cilantro
nan bread, to serve

oil   *garam masala*   *fennel seeds*

curry paste

cumin seeds

chicken breasts

tomatoes

ginger   *onion*

cilantro   *broccoli*   *garlic*

1 Remove any fat and cut the chicken into 1-inch cubes.

2 Heat the oil in a wok and fry the cumin and fennel seeds for 2 minutes, until the seeds begin to sputter. Add the onion, garlic and ginger and cook for 5–7 minutes. Stir in the curry paste and cook for another 2–3 minutes.

3 Add the broccoli florets and fry for about 5 minutes. Add the chicken cubes and fry for 5–8 minutes.

4 Add the tomatoes, garam masala and chopped cilantro. Cook for another 5–10 minutes or until the chicken is tender. Serve with nan bread.

Chicken Dopiazza

Dopiazza literally translates as "two onions" and describes this chicken dish in which two types of onions are used at different stages during the cooking process.

Serves 4

INGREDIENTS
3 tablespoons oil
8 small onions, halved
2 bay leaves
8 green cardamom pods
4 cloves
3 dried red chilies
8 black peppercorns
2 onions, finely chopped
2 garlic cloves, crushed
1-inch piece ginger root,
    finely chopped
1 teaspoon ground coriander
1 teaspoon ground cumin
½ teaspoon ground turmeric
1 teaspoon cayenne pepper
½ teaspoon salt
4 tomatoes, peeled and
    finely chopped
½ cup water
8 chicken pieces, such as thighs and
    drumsticks, skinned
plain rice, to serve

1 Heat 2 tablespoons of the oil in a large saucepan and fry the small onions for 10 minutes, or until golden brown. Remove and set aside.

2 Add the remaining oil and fry the bay leaves, cardamom, cloves, chilies and peppercorns for 2 minutes. Add the chopped onions, garlic and ginger and fry for 5 minutes. Stir in the ground spices and salt and cook for 2 minutes.

3 Add the tomatoes and the water and simmer for 5 minutes, until the sauce thickens. Add the chicken and cook for about 15 minutes.

4 Add the reserved small onions, then cover and cook for another 10 minutes, or until the chicken is tender. Serve with plain boiled rice.

COOK'S TIP
Soak the small onions in boiling water for 2–3 minutes to make them easier to peel.

cayenne pepper

ground coriander

ground cumin

black peppercorns

chicken pieces

ground turmeric

onions

tomatoes

cloves

bay leaves

garlic

cardamom pods

small onions

red chilies

ginger

Shrimp Curry

A rich flavorsome curry made from shrimp and a delicious blend of aromatic spices.

Serves 4

INGREDIENTS

1½ pounds uncooked large shrimp
4 dried red chilies
1 cup dried coconut
1 teaspoon black mustard seeds
1 large onion, chopped
3 tablespoons oil
4 bay leaves
1-inch piece ginger root,
    finely chopped
2 garlic cloves, crushed
1 tablespoon ground coriander
1 teaspoon cayenne pepper
1 teaspoon salt
4 tomatoes, finely chopped
plain rice, to serve

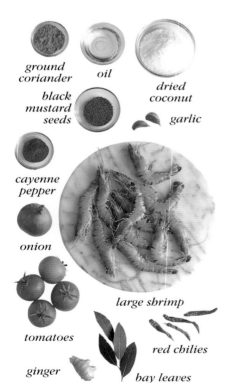

ground coriander *oil* *dried coconut*
black mustard seeds *garlic*
cayenne pepper
onion
large shrimp
tomatoes
red chilies
ginger *bay leaves*

1 Peel the shrimp. Run a sharp knife along the back of each shrimp to make a shallow cut and carefully remove the thin black intestinal vein.

2 Put the dried red chilies, coconut, mustard seeds and onion in a large frying pan and dry-fry for 8–10 minutes or until the mixture begins to brown. Put into a food processor or blender and process to a coarse paste.

3 Heat the oil in the frying pan and fry the bay leaves for 1 minute. Add the chopped ginger and the garlic and fry for 2–3 minutes.

4 Add the coriander, cayenne pepper, salt and the paste and fry for 5 minutes.

5 Stir in the chopped tomatoes and about ¾ cup water and simmer for 5–6 minutes or until thickened.

6 Add the shrimp and cook for about 4–5 minutes or until they turn pink and the edges are curling slightly. Serve with plain boiled rice.

COOK'S TIP
Serve some extra large shrimp, unpeeled, on the edge of each plate for an attractive garnish. Cook them with the peeled shrimp.

Green Fish Curry

This dish combines all the flavors of the East.

Serves 4

INGREDIENTS
¼ teaspoon ground turmeric
2 tablespoons lime juice
pinch of salt
4 cod fillets, skinned and cut into
    2-inch chunks
1 onion, chopped
1 green chili, roughly chopped
1 garlic clove, crushed
¼ cup cashew nuts
½ teaspoon fennel seeds
2 tablespoons dried coconut
2 tablespoons oil
¼ teaspoon cumin seeds
¼ teaspoon ground coriander
¼ teaspoon ground cumin
¼ teaspoon salt
⅔ cup water
¾ cup light cream
3 tablespoons finely
    chopped cilantro
Vegetable Pilaf, to serve
cilantro sprig, to garnish

light cream

lime juice

dried coconut

ground coriander

fennel seeds

ground turmeric

cashew nuts

ground cumin

onion

cod fillets

green chili

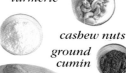

cumin seeds

cilantro

garlic

1 Mix together the turmeric, lime juice and salt and rub over the fish. Cover and let marinate for 15 minutes.

2 Meanwhile process the onion, chili, garlic, cashew nuts, fennel seeds and coconut to a paste. Spoon the paste into a bowl and set aside.

3 Heat the oil in a large frying pan and fry the cumin seeds for 2 minutes, until they begin to sputter. Add the paste and fry for 5 minutes then stir in the ground coriander, cumin, salt and water and fry for about 2–3 minutes.

4 Add the light cream and the cilantro. Simmer for 5 minutes. Add the fish and gently stir in. Cover and cook gently for 10 minutes or until the fish is tender. Serve with Vegetable Pilaf, garnished with a cilantro sprig.

Indian Fish Stew

A spicy fish stew made with potatoes, peppers and traditional Indian spices.

Serves 4

INGREDIENTS
2 tablespoons oil
1 teaspoon cumin seeds
1 onion, chopped
1 red bell pepper, thinly sliced
1 garlic clove, crushed
2 red chilies, finely chopped
2 bay leaves
½ teaspoon salt
1 teaspoon ground cumin
1 teaspoon ground coriander
1 teaspoon cayenne pepper
14-ounce can chopped tomatoes
2 large potatoes, cut into
     1-inch chunks
1¼ cups fish broth
4 cod fillets
chapatis, to serve

ground cumin

cayenne pepper

chopped tomatoes

fish broth

ground coriander

oil   *cumin seeds*

red bell pepper

onion

red chilies   *potatoes*

bay leaves

salt

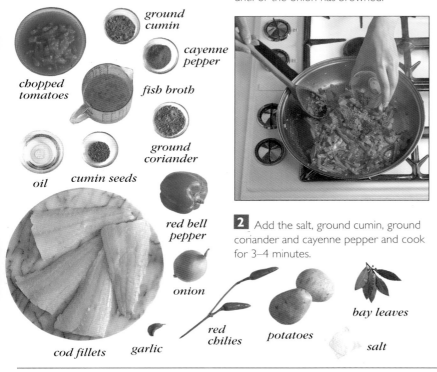

cod fillets   *garlic*

1 Heat the oil in a large deep-sided frying pan and fry the cumin seeds for 2 minutes or until they begin to sputter. Add the onion, bell pepper, garlic, chilies and bay leaves and fry for 5–7 minutes until or the onion has browned.

2 Add the salt, ground cumin, ground coriander and cayenne pepper and cook for 3–4 minutes.

3 Stir in the tomatoes, potatoes and fish broth. Bring to a boil and simmer for another 10 minutes.

4 Add the fish, then cover and simmer for 10 minutes, or until the fish is tender. Serve with chapatis.

Tunafish Curry

This unusual fish curry can be made in minutes.

Serves 4

INGREDIENTS

1 onion
1 red bell pepper
1 green bell pepper
3 tablespoons oil
¼ teaspoon cumin seeds
½ teaspoon ground cumin
½ teaspoon ground coriander
½ teaspoon cayenne pepper
¼ teaspoon salt
2 garlic cloves, crushed
12-ounce can tuna, drained
1 green chili, finely chopped
1-inch piece ginger root, grated
¼ teaspoon garam masala
1 teaspoon lemon juice
2 tablespoons chopped cilantro
pitta bread and Cucumber Raita,
   to serve
cilantro sprig, to garnish

tuna · garam masala · red bell pepper · oil · cumin seeds · green bell pepper · lemon juice · ground coriander · onion · ginger · ground cumin · cayenne pepper · green chili · salt · garlic

1 Thinly slice the onion and the red and green bell peppers.

2 Heat the oil in a large frying pan and fry the cumin seeds for 2 minutes, until they begin to sputter.

3 Add the cumin, coriander, cayenne pepper and salt; cook for 2–3 minutes. Add the garlic, onion and peppers.

4 Fry the vegetables, stirring occasionally for 5–7 minutes or until the onions have browned.

5 Stir in the tuna, chili and ginger and cook for 5 minutes.

6 Add the garam masala, lemon juice and cilantro and continue to cook for another 3–4 minutes. Serve in warmed, split pitta bread with the Cucumber Raita garnished with a cilantro sprig.

COOK'S TIP
Place the pitta bread on a broiler rack and broil until it just puffs up. It will then be easy to split with a sharp knife.

Goan-style Mussels

This is a simple way to cook mussels in a delicious fragrant coconut sauce.

Serves 4

INGREDIENTS
2 pounds live mussels
4 ounces creamed coconut
3 tablespoons oil
1 onion, finely chopped
3 garlic cloves, crushed
1-inch piece ginger root,
    finely chopped
½ teaspoon ground turmeric
1 teaspoon ground cumin
1 teaspoon ground coriander
¼ teaspoon salt
chopped cilantro, to garnish

oil

ground turmeric

ground coriander

creamed coconut

live mussels

ground cumin

onion

ginger

garlic

salt

1 Scrub the mussels in cold water and remove the beards. Discard any mussels that are already open.

2 Dissolve the creamed coconut in 1⅞ cups boiling water and set aside until needed.

3 Heat the oil in a large pan and fry the onion for 5 minutes. Add the garlic and ginger and fry for 2 minutes. Stir in the turmeric, cumin, coriander and salt and fry for another 2 minutes. Add the creamed coconut liquid, bring to a boil and simmer for 5 minutes.

4 Add the mussels, cover and cook for 6–8 minutes or until all the mussels are cooked and open. Spoon the mussels on to a serving platter and pour the sauce over, then garnish with the chopped cilantro.

Coconut Salmon

This is an ideal dish to serve at dinner parties.

Serves 4

INGREDIENTS

2 teaspoons ground cumin
2 teaspoons cayenne pepper
1/2 teaspoon ground turmeric
2 tablespoons white wine vinegar
1/4 teaspoon salt
4 salmon steaks, about
   6 ounces each
3 tablespoons oil
1 onion, chopped
2 green chilies, seeded
   and chopped
2 garlic cloves, crushed
1-inch piece ginger root, grated
1 teaspoon ground coriander
3/4 cup coconut milk
spring onion rice, to serve
cilantro sprigs, to garnish

coconut milk

oil

salmon steaks

ground coriander

ground turmeric

ground cumin

white wine vinegar

salt

onion

cayenne pepper

ginger

garlic

green chilies

1 Mix 1 teaspoon of the ground cumin together with the cayenne pepper, turmeric, vinegar and salt. Rub the paste over the salmon steaks and let marinate for about 15 minutes.

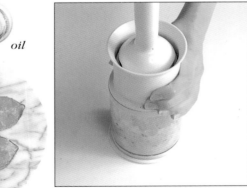

2 Heat the oil in a large deep-sided frying pan and fry the onion, chilies, garlic and ginger for 5–6 minutes. Put into a food processor or blender and process to a paste.

COOK'S TIP

If coconut milk is unavailable, dissolve some grated coconut in boiling water and strain into a measuring cup.

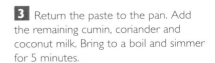

3 Return the paste to the pan. Add the remaining cumin, coriander and coconut milk. Bring to a boil and simmer for 5 minutes.

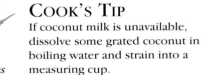

4 Add the salmon steaks. Cover and cook for 15 minutes until the fish is tender. Serve with spring onion rice and garnish with cilantro.

Fish and Okra Curry

An interesting combination of flavors and textures is used to make this delicious fish dish.

Serves 4

INGREDIENTS
1 pound monkfish
1 teaspoon ground turmeric
½ teaspoon cayenne pepper
½ teaspoon salt
1 teaspoon cumin seeds
½ teaspoon fennel seeds
2 dried red chilies
3 tablespoons oil
1 onion, finely chopped
2 garlic cloves, crushed
4 tomatoes, peeled and
   finely chopped
⅔ cup water
8 ounces okra, trimmed and cut
   into 1-inch lengths
1 teaspoon garam masala
tomato rice, to serve

fennel seeds
cumin seeds   *oil*   *ground turmeric*
garam masala
cayenne pepper
okra   *monkfish*   *tomatoes*
onion   *red chilies*

1 Remove the membrane and bones from the monkfish, cut into 1-inch cubes and place in a dish. Mix together the turmeric, cayenne pepper and ¼ teaspoon of the salt and rub all over the fish. Let marinate for 15 minutes.

2 Put the cumin seeds, fennel seeds and chilies in a large frying pan and dry-roast for 3–4 minutes. Put into a spice grinder or use a mortar and pestle and grind to a coarse powder.

3 Heat 2 tablespoons of the oil in the frying pan and and fry the fish for about 4–5 minutes. Remove with a slotted spoon and drain on paper towels.

4 Add the remaining oil to the pan and fry the onion and garlic for about 5 minutes. Add the spice powder and remaining salt and fry for 2–3 minutes. Stir in the tomatoes and water and simmer for 5 minutes.

5 Add the prepared okra and cook for about 5–7 minutes.

6 Return the fish to the pan together with the garam masala. Cover and simmer for 5–6 minutes or until the fish is tender. Serve with tomato rice.

COOK'S TIP
Yellow and plain rice would also go well with this curry, making an attractive presentation. Or serve it with plain rice, if you prefer.

Aloo Gobi

Cauliflower and potatoes are encrusted with Indian spices in this delicious recipe.

Serves 4

INGREDIENTS
1 pound potatoes, cut into
    1-inch chunks
2 tablespoons oil
1 teaspoon cumin seeds
1 green chili, finely chopped
1 pound cauliflower, broken
    into florets
1 teaspoon ground coriander
1 teaspoon ground cumin
¼ teaspoon cayenne pepper
½ teaspoon ground turmeric
½ teaspoon salt
chopped cilantro, to garnish
tomato and onion salad and pickle,
    to serve

oil

ground
coriander

cayenne
pepper

ground
cumin

cumin
seeds

ground
turmeric

cauliflower

salt

green
chili

potatoes

VARIATION
Try using sweet potatoes instead of ordinary potatoes for a tasty variation with a sweeter flavor.

1 Parboil the potatoes in a large saucepan of boiling water for 10 minutes. Drain well and set aside.

2 Heat the oil in a large frying pan and fry the cumin seeds for 2 minutes, until they begin to sputter. Add the chili and fry for another minute.

3 Add the cauliflower florets and fry, stirring, for 5 minutes.

4 Add the potatoes and the ground spices and salt and cook for another 7–10 minutes, or until both the vegetables are tender. Garnish with cilantro and serve with tomato and onion salad and pickle.

Masala Okra

Okra, or "ladies' fingers" are a popular Indian vegetable. In this recipe they are stir-fried with a dry, spicy masala to make a delicious side dish.

Serves 4

INGREDIENTS
1 pound okra
½ teaspoon ground turmeric
1 teaspoon cayenne pepper
1 tablespoon ground cumin
1 tablespoon ground coriander
¼ teaspoon salt
¼ teaspoon sugar
1 tablespoon lemon juice
1 tablespoon dried coconut
2 tablespoons chopped cilantro
3 tablespoons oil
½ teaspoon cumin seeds
½ teaspoon black mustard seeds
chopped fresh tomatoes, to garnish
poppadums, to serve

black mustard seeds
lemon juice
ground coriander
cumin seeds
ground cumin
cayenne pepper
sugar
ground turmeric
okra
dried coconut
salt
cilantro

COOK'S TIP

When buying okra, choose firm, brightly colored, unblemished pods that are less than 4 inches long.

1 Wash, dry and trim the okra. In a bowl, mix together the turmeric, cayenne pepper, cumin, ground coriander, salt, sugar, lemon juice, dried coconut and the cilantro.

2 Heat the oil in a large frying pan. Add the cumin seeds and mustard seeds and fry for about 2 minutes, or until they begin to sputter.

3 Add the spice mixture and continue to fry for 2 minutes.

4 Add the okra, cover, and cook over low heat for 10 minutes, or until tender. Garnish with chopped fresh tomatoes and serve with poppadums.

Mixed Vegetable Curry

A good all-round vegetable curry that goes well with most Indian meat dishes. You can use any combination of vegetables that are in season for this basic recipe.

Serves 4

INGREDIENTS
2 tablespoons oil
½ teaspoon black mustard seeds
½ teaspoon cumin seeds
1 onion, thinly sliced
2 curry leaves
1 green chili, finely chopped
1-inch piece ginger root,
    finely chopped
2 tablespoons curry paste
1 small cauliflower, broken
    into florets
1 large carrot, thickly sliced
4 ounces green beans, cut into
    1-inch lengths
¼ teaspoon ground turmeric
¼ teaspoon cayenne pepper
½ teaspoon salt
2 tomatoes, finely chopped
2 ounces frozen peas, thawed
⅔ cup vegetable broth
nan bread, to serve
fresh curry leaves, to garnish

curry paste *peas*
vegetable broth *black mustard seeds* *cayenne pepper*
cauliflower
ground turmeric *cumin seeds* *green beans* *carrot* *curry leaves* *onion* *green chili*
tomatoes *ginger*

1 Heat the oil in a large saucepan and fry the mustard seeds and cumin seeds for 2 minutes, until they begin to sputter.

2 Add the onion and the curry leaves and fry for 5 minutes.

3 Add the chili and ginger and fry for 2 minutes. Stir in the curry paste and fry for 3–4 minutes.

4 Add the cauliflower, carrot and green beans and cook for 4–5 minutes. Add the turmeric, cayenne pepper, salt and tomatoes and cook for 2–3 minutes.

5 Add the thawed peas and cook for another 2–3 minutes.

6 Add the broth. Cover and simmer over low heat for 10–13 minutes or until all the vegetables are tender. Serve, garnished with curry leaves.

Banana Curry

An unusual partnership, but the sweetness of bananas combines well with the spices used, producing a mild, sweet curry. Choose bananas that are slightly underripe, so that they retain their shape and do not become mushy.

Serves 4

INGREDIENTS
4 underripe bananas
2 tablespoons ground coriander
1 tablespoon ground cumin
1 teaspoon cayenne pepper
½ teaspoon salt
¼ teaspoon ground turmeric
1 teaspoon sugar
1 tablespoon gram flour
3 tablespoons chopped cilantro
6 tablespoons oil
¼ teaspoon cumin seeds
¼ teaspoon black mustard seeds
cilantro sprigs, to garnish
chapatis, to serve

oil

ground turmeric *cayenne pepper*

cumin seeds

gram flour

ground coriander

black mustard seeds

bananas

ground cumin

sugar

salt *cilantro*

1 Trim the bananas and cut each into three equal pieces, leaving the skin on. Make a lengthwise slit in each piece of banana, but don't cut right through.

2 Mix together on a plate, the coriander, cumin, cayenne pepper, salt, turmeric, sugar, gram flour, cilantro and 1 tablespoon of the oil.

3 Carefully stuff each piece of banana with the spice mixture, taking care not to break them in half.

4 Heat the remaining oil in a large heavy-based saucepan and fry the cumin and mustard seeds for 2 minutes or until they begin to sputter. Add the bananas and toss gently in the oil. Cover and simmer over low heat for 15 minutes, stirring from time to time, until the bananas are soft, but not mushy. Garnish with the cilantro sprigs and serve with warm chapatis.

Eggplant Curry

A simple and delicious way of cooking eggplant which retains their full flavor.

Serves 4

INGREDIENTS
2 large eggplant, about
    1 pound each
3 tablespoons oil
½ teaspoon black mustard seeds
1 bunch scallions,
    finely chopped
4 ounces button
    mushrooms, halved
2 garlic cloves, crushed
1 red chili, finely chopped
½ teaspoon cayenne pepper
1 teaspoon ground cumin
1 teaspoon ground coriander
¼ teaspoon ground turmeric
1 teaspoon salt
14-ounce can chopped tomatoes
1 tablespoon chopped cilantro
cilantro sprig, to garnish

black mustard seeds

cayenne pepper

ground turmeric

chopped tomatoes

ground cumin

cilantro

button mushrooms

ground coriander

eggplant

garlic

scallions

red chili

1 Preheat the oven to 400°F. Brush both of the eggplant with 1 tablespoon of the oil and prick with a fork. Bake in the oven for 30–35 minutes or until the eggplant are soft.

2 Heat the remaining oil in a saucepan and fry the mustard seeds for 2 minutes, until they begin to sputter. Add the scallions, mushrooms, garlic and chili and fry for 5 minutes. Stir in the cayenne pepper, cumin, coriander, turmeric and salt and fry for 3–4 minutes. Add the tomatoes and simmer for 5 minutes.

3 Cut each of the eggplant in half lengthwise and scoop out the soft flesh into a bowl. Mash the flesh briefly.

COOK'S TIP
If you want to omit the oil, wrap the eggplant in foil and bake in the oven for 1 hour.

4 Add the mashed eggplant and cilantro to the saucepan. Bring to a boil and simmer for 5 minutes or until the sauce thickens. Serve, garnished with a sprig of cilantro.

Corn and Pea Curry

Tender corn is cooked in a spicy tomato sauce.
Use fresh corn when it is in season.

Serves 4

INGREDIENTS
4 frozen corn on the cob, thawed
3 tablespoons oil
½ teaspoon cumin seeds
1 onion, finely chopped
2 garlic cloves, crushed
1 green chili, finely chopped
1 tablespoon curry paste
1 teaspoon ground coriander
1 teaspoon ground cumin
¼ teaspoon ground turmeric
½ teaspoon salt
½ teaspoon sugar
14-ounce can chopped tomatoes
1 tablespoon tomato paste
⅔ cup water
4 ounces frozen peas, thawed
2 tablespoons chopped
    cilantro
chapatis, to serve (optional)

peas

corn
on the cob

chopped
tomatoes

oil

sugar

tomato
paste

ground
turmeric

ground
coriander

cumin
seeds

curry paste

ground
cumin

salt

garlic

cilantro

onion

green chili

1 Use a sharp knife and cut each corn cob in quarters crossways to make 16 equal pieces in total.

2 Bring a large saucepan of water to a boil and cook the corn cob pieces for 10–12 minutes. Drain well.

3 Heat the oil in a large saucepan and fry the cumin seeds for 2 minutes or until they begin to sputter. Add the onion, garlic and chili and fry for about 5–6 minutes, until the onions are golden.

4 Add the curry paste and fry for 2 minutes. Stir in the remaining spices, salt and sugar and fry for 2–3 minutes.

5 Add the chopped tomatoes and tomato paste together with the water and simmer for 5 minutes or until the sauce thickens. Add the peas and cook for another 5 minutes.

6 Add the corn cob pieces and cilantro and cook for another 6–8 minutes or until the corn and peas are tender. Serve with chapatis, for mopping up the rich sauce, if you like.

VARIATION
If you don't like peas, you can replace them with the same quantity of frozen corn kernels.

Aloo Saag

Spinach, potatoes and traditional Indian spices are the main ingredients in this simple, delicious and authentic curry.

Serves 4

INGREDIENTS
1 pound spinach
2 tablespoons oil
1 teaspoon black mustard seeds
1 onion, thinly sliced
2 garlic cloves, crushed
1-inch piece ginger root,
    finely chopped
1½ pounds potatoes, cut into
    1-inch chunks
1 teaspoon cayenne pepper
1 teaspoon salt
1½ cup water

onion   oil

black
mustard
seeds

ginger   cayenne
pepper

spinach

salt

garlic

potatoes

1 Wash the spinach then blanch in boiling water for 3–4 minutes.

COOK'S TIP

To make certain that the spinach is dry, put it in a clean dish towel, roll up tightly and squeeze gently to remove any excess liquid.

2 Drain the spinach thoroughly and set aside. When cool enough to handle, use your hands to squeeze out any remaining liquid.

3 Heat the oil in a large saucepan and fry the mustard seeds for 2 minutes or until they begin to sputter.

4 Add the onion, garlic and ginger and fry for 5 minutes, stirring.

5 Add the potatoes, cayenne pepper, salt and water and cook for 8 minutes.

6 Add the spinach. Cover and simmer for 10–15 minutes or until the potatoes are tender. Serve hot.

COOK'S TIP
Use a waxy variety of potato for this dish so the pieces do not break up during cooking.

Mushroom Curry

This is a delicious way of cooking mushrooms which goes well with any meat dish.

Serves 4

INGREDIENTS
2 tablespoons oil
½ teaspoon cumin seeds
¼ teaspoon black peppercorns
4 green cardamom pods
¼ teaspoon ground turmeric
1 onion, finely chopped
1 teaspoon ground cumin
1 teaspoon ground coriander
½ teaspoon garam masala
1 green chili, finely chopped
2 garlic cloves, crushed
1-inch piece ginger root, grated
14-ounce can chopped tomatoes
¼ teaspoon salt
1 pound button
   mushrooms, halved
chopped cilantro, to garnish

chopped tomatoes

oil

ground turmeric

cumin seeds

black peppercorns

ground coriander

garam masala

ground cumin

onion

button mushrooms

salt

ginger

garlic

green chili

cardamom pods

1 Heat the oil in a large saucepan and fry the cumin seeds, peppercorns, cardamom pods and ground turmeric for 2–3 minutes.

2 Add the onion and fry for about 5 minutes, until golden. Stir in the cumin, coriander and garam masala and fry for another 2 minutes.

3 Add the chili, garlic and ginger and fry for 2–3 minutes, stirring constantly to prevent the spices from sticking to the pan. Add the tomatoes and salt. Bring to a boil and simmer for 5 minutes.

4 Add the mushrooms. Cover and simmer over low heat for 10 minutes. Garnish with chopped cilantro. This curry would be good with Spicy Lamb and Potato Stew.

Spicy Bitter Melons

Bitter melons are widely used in Indian cooking, both on their own and combined with other vegetables in a curry.

Serves 4

INGREDIENTS

1½ pounds bitter melons
4 tablespoons oil
½ teaspoon cumin seeds
6 scallions, finely chopped
5 tomatoes, finely chopped
1-inch piece ginger root,
    finely chopped
2 garlic cloves, crushed
2 green chilies, finely chopped
½ teaspoon salt
½ teaspoon cayenne pepper
1 teaspoon ground coriander
1 teaspoon ground cumin
3 tablespoons peanuts, crushed
3 tablespoons brown sugar
1 tablespoon gram flour
cilantro sprigs, to garnish

brown sugar   peanuts   ground cumin
ground coriander   gram flour
cumin seeds   cayenne pepper
scallions
green chilies
garlic
bitter melons
ginger   tomatoes

1 Bring a large pan of lightly salted water to a boil. Peel the bitter melons using a small sharp knife and halve them. Discard the seeds. Cut into ³/₄-inch pieces then cook in the water for about 10–15 minutes, or until they are tender. Drain well and set aside.

2 Heat the oil in a large saucepan and fry the cumin seeds for 2 minutes, until they begin to sputter. Add the scallions and fry for 3–4 minutes. Add the tomatoes, ginger, garlic and chilies and cook for 5 minutes.

3 Add the salt, remaining spices, the peanuts and sugar and cook for about 2–3 minutes.

COOK'S TIP

For a quick and easy way to crush peanuts, put into a food processor or blender and process for about 20–30 seconds.

4 Add the bitter melons and mix well. Sprinkle over the gram flour. Cover and simmer over low heat for 5–8 minutes or until all of the gram flour has been absorbed into the sauce. Serve garnished with cilantro sprigs.

Spicy French Fries with Sesame Seeds

This recipe is a variation of the well-known dish Bombay Potatoes, in which the potatoes are fried to give them a crispy texture, and then tossed in spices and sesame seeds.

Serves 4

INGREDIENTS
2 pounds potatoes
oil, for deep-frying
1/4 teaspoon ground turmeric
1/4 teaspoon cayenne pepper
1/4 teaspoon salt
2 tablespoons oil
1/4 teaspoon black mustard seeds
1 green chili, finely chopped
1 garlic clove, crushed
2 tablespoons sesame seeds

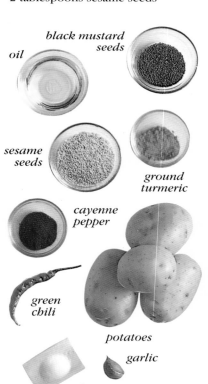

oil

black mustard seeds

sesame seeds

ground turmeric

cayenne pepper

green chili

potatoes

garlic

salt

1 Cut the potatoes into thick strips.

2 Heat the oil for deep-frying to 325°F. Fry the potatoes in batches for 5 minutes, until golden. Drain well on plenty of paper towels.

3 Put the potatoes in a bowl and sprinkle over the turmeric, cayenne pepper and salt. Cool, then toss the strips in the spices until evenly coated.

4 Heat the 2 tablespoons oil in a large saucepan and fry the mustard seeds for 2 minutes until they sputter. Add the chili and garlic and fry for 2 minutes.

5 Add the sesame seeds and fry for 3–4 minutes or until the seeds begin to brown. Remove from the heat.

6 Add the sesame seed mixture to the potatoes and toss together to coat evenly. Serve cold, or reheat for 5 minutes in an oven preheated to 400°F.

COOK'S TIP
Make sure the potato strips are as uniform in size as possible to ensure that they cook evenly.

Zucchini Curry

Thickly sliced zucchini are combined with authentic Indian spices for a delicious, colorful vegetable curry.

Serves 4

INGREDIENTS

1½ pounds zucchini
3 tablespoons oil
½ teaspoon cumin seeds
½ teaspoon mustard seeds
1 onion, thinly sliced
2 garlic cloves, crushed
¼ teaspoon ground turmeric
¼ teaspoon cayenne pepper
1 teaspoon ground coriander
1 teaspoon ground cumin
½ teaspoon salt
1 tablespoon tomato paste
14-ounce can chopped tomatoes
⅔ cup water
1 tablespoon chopped cilantro
1 teaspoon garam masala

oil *mustard seeds* *chopped tomatoes*
ground cumin *cumin seeds* *cayenne pepper*
garam masala *tomato paste* *onion*
ground turmeric *ground coriander*
salt *garlic* *zucchini*

cilantro

1 Trim the ends from the zucchini then cut into ½-inch thick slices.

2 Heat the oil in a large saucepan and fry the cumin and mustard seeds for 2 minutes or until they begin to sputte

3 Add the onion and garlic and fry for about 5–6 minutes.

4 Add the turmeric, cayenne pepper, coriander, cumin and salt and fry for about 2–3 minutes.

5 Add the sliced zucchini all at once, and cook for 5 minutes.

6 Mix together the tomato paste and chopped tomatoes and add to the saucepan with the water. Cover and simmer for 10 minutes, until the sauce thickens. Stir in the cilantro and garam masala, then cook for 5 minutes or until the zucchini are tender.

Vegetable Kashmiri

This is a delicious vegetable curry, in which fresh mixed vegetables are cooked in a spicy, aromatic yogurt sauce.

Serves 4

INGREDIENTS

2 teaspoons cumin seeds
8 black peppercorns
2 green cardamom pods, seeds only
2-inch cinnamon stick
½ teaspoon grated nutmeg
3 tablespoons oil
1 green chili, chopped
1-inch piece ginger root, grated
1 teaspoon cayenne pepper
½ teaspoon salt
2 large potatoes, cut into
    1-inch chunks
8 ounces cauliflower, broken into
    florets
8 ounces okra, thickly sliced
⅔ cup plain yogurt
⅔ cup vegetable broth
toasted flaked almonds and cilantro
    sprigs, to garnish

vegetable broth

oil

cayenne pepper

black peppercorns

cauliflower

potatoes

cumin seeds

cinnamon stick

plain yogurt

salt

nutmeg

ginger

cardamom pods

okra

green chili

1 Grind the cumin seeds, peppercorns, cardamom seeds, cinnamon stick and nutmeg to a fine powder using a mortar and pestle or spice grinder.

2 Heat the oil in a large saucepan and fry the chili and ginger for 2 minutes, stirring all the time.

3 Add the cayenne pepper, salt and ground spice mixture and fry for about 2–3 minutes, stirring constantly to prevent the spices from sticking.

4 Stir in the potatoes, cover, and cook for 10 minutes over low heat, stirring from time to time.

5 Add the cauliflower and okra and cook for 5 minutes.

6 Add the yogurt and broth. Bring to a boil, then reduce the heat. Cover and simmer for 20 minutes, or until all the vegetables are tender. Garnish with toasted almonds and cilantro sprigs.

Stuffed Baby Vegetables

The combination of potatoes and eggplant is popular in Indian cooking. This recipe uses small, baby vegetables which are stuffed with a dry, spicy masala paste.

Serves 4

INGREDIENTS
12 small potatoes
8 small eggplant

FOR THE STUFFING
1 tablespoon sesame seeds
2 tablespoons ground coriander
2 tablespoons ground cumin
1/2 teaspoon salt
1/4 teaspoon cayenne pepper
1/2 teaspoon ground turmeric
2 teaspoons sugar
1/4 teaspoon garam masala
1 tablespoon peanuts,
    roughly crushed
1 tablespoon gram flour
2 garlic cloves, crushed
1 tablespoon lemon juice
2 tablespoons chopped cilantro

FOR THE SAUCE
2 tablespoons oil
1/2 teaspoon black mustard seeds
14-ounce can chopped tomatoes
2 tablespoons chopped cilantro
2/3 cup water
light cream, to garnish (optional)

1 Preheat the oven to 400°F. Make slits in the potatoes and eggplant, but take care not to cut all the way through.

2 Mix all the ingredients for the stuffing together on a plate.

3 Carefully stuff the potatoes and eggplant with the spice mixture.

chopped tomatoes

small eggplant

oil

peanuts

garam masala

ground turmeric

sesame seeds

black mustard seeds

cayenne pepper

gram flour

sugar

ground coriander

cilantro

salt

small potatoes

garlic

lemon juice

ground cumin

4 Place the potatoes and eggplant in a greased casserole.

5 Heat the oil in a saucepan and fry the mustard seeds for 2 minutes, until they begin to sputter, then add the tomatoes, cilantro and any leftover stuffing together with the water. Simmer for 5 minutes, until the sauce thickens.

6 Pour the sauce over the potatoes and eggplant. Cover and bake for 25–30 minutes until the potatoes and eggplant are soft. Garnish the vegetables with light cream, if using.

Chicken Biryani

Biryanis originated in Persia and are traditionally made with meat and rice. They are often served at dinner parties and on festive occasions.

Serves 4

INGREDIENTS

1½ cups basmati rice
2 tablespoons oil
1 onion, thinly sliced
2 garlic cloves, crushed
1 green chili, finely chopped
1-inch piece of ginger root, finely chopped
1½ pounds chicken breasts, skinned and cut into 1-inch cubes
3 tablespoons curry paste
¼ teaspoon salt
¼ teaspoon garam masala
3 tomatoes, cut into thin wedges
¼ teaspoon ground turmeric
2 bay leaves
4 cardamom pods
4 cloves
¼ teaspoon saffron strands
Tomato and Chili Chutney, to serve
cilantro, to garnish

garam masala
ground turmeric
curry paste
basmati rice
oil
chicken breasts
bay leaves
onion
tomatoes
saffron strands
ginger
cloves
cardamom pods
salt
green chili
garlic

1 Wash the rice in several changes of cold water. Put into a large bowl, cover with plenty of cold water and let soak for 30 minutes.

2 Meanwhile, heat the oil in a large frying pan and fry the onion for about 5–7 minutes, until lightly browned. Add the garlic, chili and ginger and fry for about 2 minutes.

3 Add the chicken and fry for about 5 minutes, stirring occasionally.

4 Add the curry paste, salt and garam masala and cook for 5 minutes. Add the tomatoes and continue to cook for another 3–4 minutes. Remove from the heat and set aside.

5 Preheat the oven to 375°F. Bring a large saucepan of water to a boil. Drain the rice and add it to the pan with the turmeric. Cook for about 10 minutes, or until the rice is almost tender. Drain the rice and toss together with the bay leaves, cardamom pods, cloves and saffron.

6 Layer the rice and chicken in a shallow casserole until all the mixture has been used, finishing off with a layer of rice. Cover and bake in the oven for 15–20 minutes, or until the chicken is tender. Serve with Tomato and Chili Chutney, garnished with cilantro.

VARIATION

For a vegetarian dish replace the chicken with 1 pound mixed vegetables, such as cauliflower, carrots, peas and green beans. Choose vegetables that have contrasting colors and textures.

Kidney Bean Curry

This a very popular Punjabi-style dish using red kidney beans, but you can substitute the same quantity of lima beans, if you prefer.

Serves 4

INGREDIENTS

1¼ cups dried red kidney beans
2 tablespoons oil
½ teaspoon cumin seeds
1 onion, thinly sliced
1 green chili, finely chopped
2 garlic cloves, crushed
1-inch piece ginger root, grated
2 tablespoons curry paste
1 teaspoon ground cumin
1 teaspoon ground coriander
½ teaspoon cayenne pepper
½ teaspoon salt
14-ounce can chopped tomatoes
2 tablespoons chopped cilantro

chopped tomatoes

oil

curry paste

cayenne pepper

ground coriander

red kidney beans

ground cumin

cumin seeds

garlic

salt   onion

green chili

cilantro

ginger

1 Place the red kidney beans in a large bowl of cold water then let them soak overnight.

2 Drain the beans and place in a large saucepan with double their volume of water. Boil rapidly for 10 minutes. Skim off any scum. Cover and cook for 1–1½ hours, or until the beans are soft.

COOK'S TIP
If you want to reduce the cooking time, cook the beans in a pressure cooker for 20–25 minutes.

3 Meanwhile, heat the oil in a large frying pan and fry the cumin seeds for 2 minutes, until they begin to sputter. Add the onion, chili, garlic and ginger and fry for 5 minutes. Stir in the curry paste, cumin, coriander, cayenne pepper and salt and cook for 5 minutes.

4 Add the tomatoes and simmer for 5 minutes. Add the beans and cilantro, reserving a little for the garnish. Cover and cook for 15 minutes adding a little water if necessary. Serve, garnished with the reserved cilantro.

Spinach Dal

There are many different types of dals eaten in India, with each region having its own specialty. This is a delicious, lightly spiced dish with a nutty flavor from the channa dal or split peas, which combine well with spinach.

Serves 4

INGREDIENTS
1 cup channa dal or yellow
  split peas
¾ cup water
2 tablespoons oil
¼ teaspoon black mustard seeds
1 onion, thinly sliced
2 garlic cloves, crushed
1-inch piece ginger root, grated
1 red chili, finely chopped
10 ounces frozen spinach, thawed
¼ teaspoon cayenne pepper
½ teaspoon ground coriander
½ teaspoon garam masala
½ teaspoon salt

channa dal

ground coriander

garam masala

cayenne pepper

spinach

salt

onion

garlic

oil

black mustard seeds

ginger

red chili

1 Wash the channa dal or split peas in several changes of cold water. Put into a bowl and cover with plenty of water. Set aside to soak for 30 minutes.

2 Drain the channa dal or split peas and put in a large saucepan with the water. Bring to a boil, cover, and simmer for 20–25 minutes or until soft.

3 Meanwhile, heat the oil in a large frying pan and fry the mustard seeds for 2 minutes, until they begin to sputter. Add the onion, garlic, ginger and chili and fry for 5–6 minutes. Add the spinach and cook for 10 minutes or until the spinach is dry and the liquid has been absorbed. Stir in the remaining spices and salt and cook for 2–3 minutes.

4 Drain the channa dal or split peas, add to the spinach and cook for about 5 minutes. Serve at once.

Masala Channa

Chick-peas are used and cooked in a variety of ways all over the Indian sub-continent. Tamarind gives this dish a deliciously sharp, tangy flavor.

COOK'S TIP

To save time, make double the quantity of tamarind pulp and freeze in ice-cube trays. It will keep for up to 2 months.

Serves 4

INGREDIENTS
1¼ cups dried chick-peas
¼ cup tamarind pulp
½ cup boiling water
3 tablespoons oil
½ teaspoon cumin seeds
1 onion, finely chopped
2 garlic cloves, crushed
1-inch piece ginger root, grated
1 green chili, finely chopped
1 teaspoon ground cumin
1 teaspoon ground coriander
¼ teaspoon ground turmeric
½ teaspoon salt
4 tomatoes, peeled and
    finely chopped
½ teaspoon garam masala
chopped chilies and chopped
    onion, to garnish

oil

tamarind pulp

chick-peas

tomatoes

ground cumin

ground coriander

onion

cumin seeds

ground turmeric

ginger

green chili

garam masala

salt

1 Put the chick-peas in a large bowl and cover with plenty of cold water. Set aside to soak overnight.

2 Drain the chick-peas and place in a large saucepan with double their volume of cold water. Bring to a boil and boil rapidy for 10 minutes. Skim off any scum. Cover and simmer for 1½–2 hours or until the chick-peas are soft.

3 Meanwhile, break up the tamarind and soak in the boiling water for about 15 minutes. Rub the tamarind through a strainer into a bowl, discarding any stones and fiber.

4 Heat the oil in a large saucepan and fry the cumin seeds for 2 minutes, until they sputter. Add the onion, garlic, ginger and chili and fry for 5 minutes.

5 Add the cumin, coriander, turmeric and salt and fry for 3–4 minutes. Add the tomatoes and tamarind pulp. Bring to a boil and simmer for 5 minutes.

6 Add the chick-peas and garam masala. Cover and simmer for about 15 minutes. Garnish with chopped chilies and onion.

Lentils and Rice

Lentils are cooked with whole and ground spices, potatoes, rice and onions to produce an authentic Indian-style risotto.

Serves 4

INGREDIENTS
¾ cup red split lentils
½ cup basmati rice
1 large potato
1 large onion
2 tablespoons oil
4 whole cloves
¼ teaspoon cumin seeds
¼ teaspoon ground turmeric
2 teaspoons salt
1¼ cups water

basmati rice

oil

cumin seeds

ground turmeric

red split lentils

potato

salt

onion

cloves

1 Wash the red split lentils and rice in several changes of cold water. Put into a bowl and cover with water. Let soak for 15 minutes then drain.

2 Peel then cut the potato into 1-inch chunks.

3 Thinly slice the onion.

4 Heat the oil in a large heavy-bottomed saucepan and fry the cloves and cumin seeds for 2 minutes, until the seeds are beginning to sputter.

5 Add the onion and potatoes and fry for 5 minutes. Add the lentils, rice, turmeric and salt and fry for 3 minutes.

6 Add the water. Bring to a boil, cover and simmer for 15–20 minutes, until all the water has been absorbed and the potatoes are tender. Let stand, covered, for about 10 minutes before serving.

Mung Beans with Potatoes

Mung beans are one of the quicker-cooking beans which do not require soaking and are therefore very easy to use. In this recipe they are cooked with potatoes and traditional Indian spices to give a tasty nutritious dish.

Serves 4

INGREDIENTS
1 cup mung beans
3 cups water
8 ounces potatoes, cut into
    ³⁄₄-inch chunks
2 tablespoons oil
½ teaspoon cumin seeds
1 green chili, finely chopped
1 garlic clove, crushed
1-inch piece ginger root,
    finely chopped
¼ teaspoon ground turmeric
½ teaspoon cayenne pepper
1 teaspoon salt
1 teaspoon sugar
4 curry leaves
5 tomatoes, peeled and
    finely chopped
1 tablespoon tomato paste
curry leaves, to garnish
plain rice, to serve

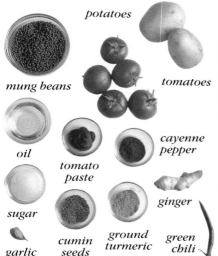

potatoes

mung beans

tomatoes

oil

tomato paste

cayenne pepper

sugar

ginger

garlic

cumin seeds

ground turmeric

green chili

curry leaves

salt

1 Wash the beans. Bring to a boil in the water, cover and simmer until soft, about 30 minutes. Parboil the potatoes for 10 minutes in another saucepan, then drain well.

2 Heat the oil and fry the cumin seeds, until they sputter. Add the chili, garlic and ginger and fry for 3–4 minutes.

3 Add the turmeric, cayenne pepper, salt and sugar and cook for 2 minutes, stirring to prevent the mixture from sticking to the saucepan.

4 Add the curry leaves, tomatoes and tomato paste and simmer for 5 minutes, until the sauce thickens. Add the tomato sauce and potatoes to the mung beans and mix together. Serve with plain boiled rice, and garnish with curry leaves.

Madras Sambal

There are many variations of this dish but it is regularly cooked in one form or another in almost every south-Indian home and served as part of a meal. You can use any combination of vegetables in season.

Serves 4

INGREDIENTS
1 cup yellow lentils
2½ cups water
½ teaspoon ground turmeric
2 large potatoes, cut into
    1-inch chunks
2 tablespoons oil
½ teaspoon black mustard seeds
¼ teaspoon fenugreek seeds
4 curry leaves
1 onion, thinly sliced
4 ounces green beans, cut
    into 1-inch lengths
1 teaspoon salt
½ teaspoon cayenne pepper
1 tablespoon lemon juice
4 tablespoons dried coconut
toasted coconut, to garnish
Cilantro Chutney, to serve

yellow lentils
black mustard seeds
ground turmeric
fenugreek seeds
dried coconut
potatoes
cayenne pepper
lemon juice
curry leaves
onion
green beans

1 Wash the lentils in several changes of cold water. Place in a large heavy-bottomed saucepan with the water and turmeric. Cover tightly and simmer for 30–35 minutes, until the lentils are soft.

2 Parboil the potatoes in a large pan of boiling water for 10 minutes. Drain well and set aside.

3 Heat the oil in a large frying pan and fry the mustard seeds, fenugreek seeds and curry leaves for 2–3 minutes, until the seeds begin to sputter. Add the onion and the green beans and fry for 7–8 minutes. Add the potatoes and cook for another 2 minutes.

4 Stir in the the lentils with the salt, cayenne pepper and lemon juice and simmer for 2 minutes. Stir in the coconut and simmer for 5 minutes. Garnish with toasted coconut and serve with freshly made Cilantro Chutney.

Mixed Bean Curry

You can use any combination of beans that you have in the storecupboard for this recipe.

Serves 4

INGREDIENTS
⅓ cup red kidney beans
⅓ cup black-eyed peas
⅓ cup navy beans
⅓ cup small cannellini beans
2 tablespoons oil
1 teaspoon cumin seeds
1 teaspoon black mustard seeds
1 onion, finely chopped
2 garlic cloves, crushed
1-inch piece ginger root, grated
2 green chilies, finely chopped
2 tablespoons curry paste
½ teaspoon salt
14-ounce can chopped tomatoes
2 tablespoons tomato paste
1 cup water
2 tablespoons chopped cilantro
chopped cilantro, to garnish

2 Drain the beans and put into a large heavy-based saucepan with double their volume of cold water. Boil rapidly for 10 minutes. Skim off any scum. Cover and simmer for 1½ hours or until the beans are soft.

black mustard seeds

chopped tomatoes

curry paste

cumin seeds

oil

black-eyed peas

red kidney beans

onion

tomato paste

navy beans

small cannellini beans

ginger

green chilies

cilantro

garlic

1 Put the beans in a large bowl and cover with plenty of cold water. Let soak overnight, mixing occasionally.

3 Heat the oil in a large saucepan and fry the cumin seeds and mustard seeds for 2 minutes, until the seeds begin to sputter. Add the onion, garlic, ginger and chili and fry for 5 minutes.

4 Add the curry paste and fry for another 2–3 minutes, stirring, then add the salt.

5 Add the tomatoes, tomato paste and the water and simmer for 5 minutes.

90

6 Add the drained beans and the cilantro. Cover and simmer for about 30–40 minutes, until the sauce thickens and the beans are cooked. Garnish with chopped cilantro.

COOK'S TIP
Depending on the types of beans you use, you may need to adjust the cooking time.

Egg and Lentil Curry

A few Indian spices can transform eggs and lentils into a tasty, economical curry.

Serves 4

INGREDIENTS

⅓ cup green lentils
3 cups vegetable broth
6 eggs
2 tablespoons oil
3 cloves
¼ teaspoon black peppercorns
1 onion, finely chopped
2 green chilies, finely chopped
2 garlic cloves, crushed
1-inch piece ginger root,
    finely chopped
2 tablespoons curry paste
14-ounce can chopped tomatoes
½ teaspoon sugar
½ teaspoon garam masala

vegetable broth

chopped tomatoes

green lentils

onion

green chili

oil

curry paste

ginger

garlic

cloves

sugar

garam masala

eggs

black peppercorns

1 Wash the lentils under cold running water, checking for small stones. Put in a large heavy-bottomed saucepan with the broth. Cover and simmer gently for about 15 minutes or until the lentils are soft. Drain and set aside.

2 Cook the eggs in boiling water for 10 minutes. When cool enough to handle, peel and cut in half lengthwise.

3 Heat the oil in a large saucepan and fry the cloves and peppercorns for about 2 minutes. Add the onion, chilies, garlic and ginger and fry the mixture for another 5-6 minutes.

4 Stir in the curry paste and fry for 2 minutes.

5 Stir in the tomatoes and sugar with ³/₄ cup water.

6 Simmer for 5 minutes until the sauce thickens. Add the eggs, drained lentils and garam masala. Cover and simmer for about 10 minutes, then serve.

Vegetable Pilaf

A popular vegetable rice dish that goes well with most Indian meat dishes.

Serves 4–6

INGREDIENTS
1 cup basmati rice
2 tablespoons oil
½ teaspoon cumin seeds
2 bay leaves
4 cardamom pods
4 cloves
1 onion, finely chopped
1 carrot, finely diced
½ cup frozen peas, thawed
⅓ cup frozen corn
    kernels, thawed
1 ounce cashew nuts, lightly fried
2 cups water
¼ teaspoon ground cumin
¼ teaspoon ground coriander
½ teaspoon salt

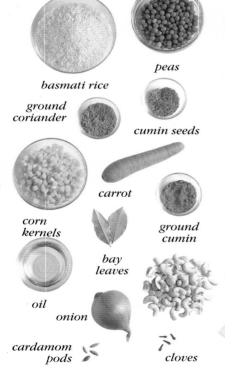

basmati rice

peas

ground coriander

cumin seeds

carrot

corn kernels

ground cumin

bay leaves

cashew nuts

oil

onion

cardamom pods

cloves

salt

1 Wash the basmati rice in several changes of cold water. Put into a bowl and cover with water. Set aside to soak for 30 minutes.

2 Heat the oil in a large frying pan and fry the cumin seeds for 2 minutes. Add the bay leaves, cardamom pods and cloves and fry for 2 minutes.

3 Add the onion and fry for 5 minutes, until lightly browned.

4 Stir in the carrot and cook for 3–4 minutes.

5 Drain the rice and add to the pan with the peas, corn and cashew nuts. Fry for 4–5 minutes.

6 Add the water, remaining spices and salt. Bring to a boil, cover, and simmer for 15 minutes over low heat, until all the water is absorbed. Allow to stand, covered, for 10 minutes before serving.

INDEX